Travel Guide To

Regensburg, GERMANY

"Where History Meets Modern Marvels – Your Perfect Escape!"

Wybikes Hinton

COPYRIGHT NOTICE

This publication is copyright protected. This is only for personal use. No part of this publication may be, including but not limited to, reproduced, in any form or medium, stored in a data retrieval system or transmitted by or through any means, without prior written permission from the Author / Publisher.

Legal action will be pursued if this is breached.

DISCLAIMER

Please note that the information contained within this document is for educational purposes only. The information contained herein has been obtained from sources believed to be reliable at the time of publication. The opinions expressed herein are subject to change without notice.

Readers acknowledge that the Author / Publisher is not engaging in rendering legal, financial or professional advice. The Publisher / Author disclaims all warranties as to the accuracy, completeness, or adequacy of such information.

The Publisher assumes no liability for errors, omissions, or inadequacies in the information contained herein or from the interpretations thereof. The publisher / Author specifically disclaims any liability from the use or application of the information contained herein or from the interpretations thereof.

TABLE OF CONTENT

Copyright Notice
Disclaimer
Table of Content
Introduction
Welcome To Regensburg, Germany!

About This Travel Guide

Why Regensburg?

How To Use This Guide

Chapter 1
Planning Your Trip To Regensburg

Best Time To Visit

How To Go To Regensburg

Visa Requirements (If applicable)

Transportation Within The City

Currency And Money Matters

Chapter 2
Getting Around Regensburg

Public Transportation

Walking Tours

Bike Rentals

Chapter 3
Top Tourist Attractions In Regensburg

Regensburg Cathedral (Dom. St. Peter)

Old Stone Bridge (Steinerne Brücke)

Thurn Und Taxis Palace

Walhalla Memorial

Saint Emmeram's Abbey (Schloss Thurn Und Taxis)

Historical Wurstkuchl

Altes Rathaus (The Old Town Hall)

Danube River Cruises

Regensburg Museum Of History

Document Neupfarrplatz (Dokumentationszentrum Reichsparteitagsgelände)

Chapter 4
Exploring Regensburg's Old Town

Discovering Hidden Gems

Shopping In Old Town Markets

Trying Local Cuisine

Chapter 5
Outdoor Activities In and Around Regensburg

Hiking In The Bavarian Forest

Cycling Along The Danube

Danube River Activities (Canoeing, Kayaking, etc.)

Parks And Gardens In Regensburg

Chapter 6
Cultural Experiences In Regensburg

Attend A Classical Concert

Visit Local Art Galleries And Museums

Festival And Event Calendar

Chapter 7
Day Trips From Regensburg

Weltenburg Abbey And Danube Gorge

Nuremberg

Munich

Salzburg, Austria

Neuschwanstein Castle

Chapter 8
What To Do In Regensburg

Join A Guided Walking Tour

Visit A Beer Garden

Attend A Traditional Bavarian Event

Explore Regensburg's Nightlife

Chapter 9
What Not To Do In Regensburg

Disrespect Local Customs And Traditions

Ignore Public Transportation Rules

Litter Or Damage Historic Sites

Overlook Safety Precautions

Chapter 10
Essential Tips For Visitors

Learn Basic German Phrases

Respect Quiet Hours

Carry Cash For Smaller Purchase

Stay Hydrated And Sun Protected

Chapter 11
Itineraries For Different Kinds Of Travelers

Weekend Getaway

Cultural Immersion

Outdoor Adventure

Family-Friendly Trip

Budget Travel

Chapter 12
Accommodation

Overview Of Accommodation Options

Luxury Resorts

Budget-Friendly Hotels

Top Recommended Hotels And Resorts

Choosing The Right Accommodation For You

Bookkeeping Tips & Tricks

Conclusion

Recap Of Regensburg Highlights

Farewell And Happy Travels

Appendix: Useful Resources

A. Emergency Contacts

Tourist Information Center

B. Maps And Navigational Tools

City Maps

C. Additional Reading And References

D. Useful Local Phrases

INTRODUCTION

WELCOME TO REGENSBURG, GERMANY!

Welcome to Regensburg, a city rich in history, culture, and charm. Regensburg, located on the banks of the Danube River in Bavaria, Germany, is a gorgeous site that provides tourists a look into its rich history while simultaneously embracing modernity.

Regensburg, with its well-preserved medieval buildings, bustling arts scene, and exquisite gastronomy, has something for everyone.

About This Travel Guide

This travel book is an important companion for seeing everything Regensburg has to offer. Whether you're a history buff hoping to meander through cobblestone alleys lined with centuries-old buildings or a foodie looking to sample Bavarian delicacies, this guide is designed to help you make the most of your trip.

Inside, you'll discover in-depth information on the city's main attractions, eating recommendations, lodging alternatives, transit tips, and more. Whether you're planning a weekend break or a prolonged stay, this guide will help you organize the perfect trip to Regensburg.

Why Regensburg?

Regensburg's attractiveness stems from its unique combination of history, culture, and natural beauty. Regensburg, one of Germany's best-preserved medieval cities, with a UNESCO World Heritage-listed Old Town replete with architectural marvels including the renowned Stone Bridge and the magnificent Regensburg Cathedral.

Aside from its historical sites, Regensburg has a strong cultural scene, with museums, galleries, and theatres displaying the city's creative past. Regensburg hosts a variety of events, from classical concerts to contemporary art exhibitions, that will engage visitors of all interests.

Furthermore, Regensburg's position along the scenic Danube River makes it an excellent choice for outdoor enthusiasts. Whether you're exploring the city on foot or taking a picturesque river cruise, Regensburg's stunning architecture and surrounding countryside never fail to please.

In addition to its cultural and natural features, Regensburg is noted for its friendly people and active environment. With lovely cafés, busy markets, and traditional beer gardens, the city provides several possibilities to immerse yourself in Bavarian culture and interact with people.

Overall, Regensburg's combination of history, culture, and natural beauty makes it a must-see destination for anyone looking for a genuine German experience.

How To Use This Guide

This guide is intended to be user-friendly and simple to use, so you can easily discover the information you need to organize your trip to Regensburg. Here's a quick summary of how to get the most out of this guide:

1. Explore Top Attractions: Learn about the must-see sites and attractions that distinguish Regensburg.

2. Dining Recommendations: Sample Bavarian cuisine at the city's top restaurants, cafés, and beer gardens.

3. Accommodation Options: Find the ideal location to stay, whether you're looking for a luxurious hotel, a nice guesthouse, or a low-cost hostel.

4. Transportation Tips: Use our transportation guidelines to easily navigate the city, including instructions for taking public transportation, biking, or walking.

5. Day Trips & Excursions: With our day trip and excursion options, you may get out of the city and explore the surrounding area.

6. Practical Information: Get useful travel ideas and recommendations, such as money, language, and safety.

By following the advice in this book, you'll be well-prepared to enjoy everything Regensburg has to offer and make experiences that will last a lifetime. So pack your luggage, ready to be fascinated by Regensburg's elegance, and set off on a memorable tour around this intriguing city.

CHAPTER 1

PLANNING YOUR TRIP TO REGENSBURG

Regensburg is a city that has captivated my heart with its medieval beauty and dynamic vitality.

As a seasoned tourist who has spent many hours exploring its cobblestone streets and ancient sites, I'm eager to share my tips for organizing the ideal vacation to this lovely German location.

So, let us delve in and discover the keys to make your Regensburg journey unique.

Best Time To Visit

Picture this: it's a beautiful autumn morning, and the leaves are blazing in gold and scarlet as you walk down the Danube River, appreciating the city's timeless elegance. Perhaps the festive atmosphere of Regensburg's Christmas markets entices you to visit during the winter months, when the perfume of mulled wine and gingerbread fills the air. Regensburg has something spectacular to offer at any time of year.

May through September are good months for visitors looking for pleasant weather and less crowds. Summer provides pleasant weather and long, bright days, ideal for visiting outdoor sights like the majestic Walhalla Memorial or enjoying a leisurely boat tour along the Danube. Just make sure you bring sunscreen and a hat to remain cool at the peak of the summer heat.

If you enjoy festive festivals and traditional Bavarian culture, try visiting during the winter holiday season. Regensburg transforms into a winter paradise from late November to December, complete with glittering lights and festive decorations. Don't miss out on sampling seasonal goodies like roasted chestnuts and delicious bratwurst while strolling around the city's lovely Christmas markets.

How To Go To Regensburg

Now let's speak about logistics. Regensburg is more accessible than you may expect, due to its central location and well-connected transit network. If you're coming from overseas, Munich International Airport (MUC) is your entryway to Bavaria, located around 80 miles south of Regensburg.

Regensburg is accessible via numerous modes of transportation from Munich Airport. Trains are the most convenient and fastest mode of transportation, with direct connections departing from the airport's train station on a regular basis. Board an InterCity Express (ICE) or Regional Express (RE) train going for Regensburg Hauptbahnhof (major rail station) and enjoy a magnificent ride through the Bavarian countryside.

Regensburg's Hauptbahnhof serves as a significant transportation center, with regular arrivals and departures from other German cities and surrounding countries. From here, it's only a short walk or tram ride to the city center, where your Regensburg journey begins.

Visa Requirements (If applicable)

Before you pack your bags and go for Regensburg, be sure you have the necessary visa to enter Germany.

Fortunately, citizens of several countries, including the United States, Canada, and the European Union, can enter Germany without a visa for short periods of up to 90 days for leisure or business.

However, if you want to remain for a lengthy period of time or are going from a nation that requires a visa for admission, you should get the proper papers well in advance of your journey.

Contact the German consulate or embassy in your home country to learn about visa requirements and application procedures, and make sure to leave plenty of time for processing.

Transportation Within The City

Once you've arrived in Regensburg, you'll discover that moving around the city is simple due to its small size and good public transit system.

The majority of the city's prominent attractions are within walking distance of one another, making it simple to explore by foot and take up the ambiance of this old city.

Regensburg has a robust network of buses and trams run by RVV (Regensburger Verkehrsverbund) for longer trips or to access far-flung destinations.

Purchase a day pass or single tickets from vending machines at tram stations or on buses, then climb onboard to explore everything Regensburg has to offer.

If you want to explore at your own leisure, try hiring a bicycle from one of the city's many bike rental businesses. Cycling is a practical and eco-friendly way to get about Regensburg, with dedicated bike lanes and bike-friendly infrastructure.

You may also enjoy the fresh air and gorgeous sights.

Currency And Money Matters

Money--an vital component of every travel journey. Regensburg's currency is the Euro (€), which is widely accepted at hotels, restaurants, stores, and tourist attractions across the city. Be careful to bring a combination of cash and credit/debit cards for convenience, as some smaller restaurants may only accept cash.

When it comes to converting cash, Regensburg's city center has lots of alternatives, including banks, exchange offices and ATMs. While ATMs are widely available, be aware of the potential costs connected with currency translation and overseas withdrawals, and consider informing your bank of your trip intentions in advance to minimize card usage complications abroad.

As you begin on your vacation in Regensburg, remember to budget sensibly and make the most of your travel expenditures by prioritizing the activities that are most important to you. Every time spent in Regensburg is guaranteed to be memorable, whether it's enjoying a wonderful Bavarian dinner at a local pub, appreciating panoramic views from the famed Stone Bridge, or just indulging in a scoop of creamy gelato from a charming gelateria.

To summarize, organizing a vacation to Regensburg is a thrilling undertaking with many options and discoveries to be made. From determining the best time to visit to managing transportation and financial issues, this lovely Bavarian city welcomes visitors from near and far. So pack your luggage, plan your excursion, and prepare to go on an incredible tour through Regensburg's legendary streets.

CHAPTER 2

GETTING AROUND REGENSBURG

Getting about Regensburg is like dancing through time and cobblestone streets. Allow me to lead you through the charming forms of transportation that will smoothly weave you into the historical fabric of this medieval treasure.

Public Transportation

Regensburg's transportation rhythm is clearly driven by its well-organized public transit infrastructure. Consider this: you get aboard a vintage tram, its rhythmic clatter echoing stories from the past, and you find yourself flying through the city's small alleyways and big squares. The Regensburger Verkehrsverbund (RVV) guarantees that this symphony of movement is both efficient and enjoyable.

Buses and trams, painted burgundy and cream, crisscross

the city, linking its numerous areas like threads in a finely woven tapestry. The Hauptbahnhof, Regensburg's major train station, serves as a lively intersection, bringing numerous pathways together to take you on experiences in the heart of the city.

For the detail-oriented visitor, each trip on these trams becomes a moving panorama. As you pass, the medieval façade tell stories and show glimpses of architectural masterpieces like as the Alte Kapelle and the Rathaus. It's more than simply a commute; it's a voyage through time, allowing you to experience the peaceful coexistence of history and modernity.

And oh, the delight of uncovering hidden jewels as you exit at various stops! The RVV network easily connects you to sights such as the ancient Porta Praetoria and the peaceful Stadtamhof neighborhood on the opposite bank of the Danube. With well-marked routes and schedules, traveling Regensburg is a snap, allowing you to enjoy every second of your adventures.

Walking Tours

Now, let us put on our comfy shoes and begin on an adventure that goes beyond basic transportation: the art of strolling through Regensburg's winding streets. Walking tours in this city are more than just getting to your goal; they're a languid waltz through the pages of history, with each step revealing a new narrative.

The allure of walking around the UNESCO World Heritage-listed Old Town is unrivaled. The ancient alleyways, with half-timbered buildings standing shoulder to shoulder, transport you to a bygone period. As you walk on the cobblestones, worn by centuries of footfall, echoes of the past fill the air.

Engage the services of an experienced local guide or follow well-marked maps, and you'll be immersed in the stories of Regensburg's golden period. The magnificent Dom St. Peter, with its twin spires piercing the sky, is a tribute to centuries of architectural excellence. Wander around the Haidplatz plaza, where the Altes Rathaus (Old Town Hall) proudly overlooks the bustling market below.

The beauty of a walking tour is found not just in the grandeur of landmarks, but also in personal contacts with the city's pulse. Pause in a modest café buried away in a secret nook, enjoy a cup of freshly brewed coffee, and let Regensburg's rhythm to permeate into your spirit. Admire street entertainers, peruse unusual stores, and get lost in the unplanned moments that turn every step into an experience.

Consider exploring beyond the well-trodden streets into the Stadtamhof neighborhood, which is divided from the Old Town by the old Stone Bridge. The speed slows here, and the tranquility of the riverbed encourages introspection. The Thurn und Taxis Palace, a royal presence above the Danube, provides an air of aristocratic refinement to your walking tour.

Bike Rentals

As the sun shines warmly over Regensburg, consider joining the city's bicycle-friendly community. Rent a bike, and you'll find yourself in a different tempo, combining with the bright energy of this bustling Bavarian town. Cycling around Regensburg is more than simply a mode of transportation; it's a proclamation of liberty, a passport to explore the city at your leisure.

Numerous bike rental businesses dot the city, offering a wide range of alternatives, from antique cruisers to sleek electric cycles. Once mounted, peddle around the city's dedicated bike lanes, which connect historic sites to verdant riverfront walks. The freedom of the wide road, or, in this instance, the open bike lane, is yours to enjoy.

One of the benefits of riding in Regensburg is the opportunity to cover more land while still enjoying the finer nuances. Glide by the majestic walls of the Stadtamhof, feel the wind whispering Danube tales, and bask in the sensation of emancipation as you bike beneath the arches of the Stone Bridge.

For the daring, consider taking a bike ride outside of the municipal limits. Follow the Danube Cycle Path, a lovely path that passes through beautiful scenery and quaint villages. Each pedal stroke becomes a brushstroke, creating a vibrant canvas of the Bavarian landscape.

Regensburg's commitment to cycling is exemplified by its unique "RadlBus" service, which allows you to combine riding with longer travels on buses equipped with bike racks. This creative technique smoothly blends several forms of transportation, resulting in a delicious blend of convenience and adventure.

To summarize, traveling about Regensburg is more than simply a logistical conundrum; it's a story braided with strands of history, culture, and the pure delight of exploring. Whether you select the rhythmic dance of trams, the quiet saunter of walking tours, or the liberated ride of a bicycle, each mode of transportation adds a brushstroke to your Regensburg experience painting.

So, put on your walking shoes, buy a tram ticket, or hire a bike, and let the adventure through Regensburg unfold one delicious stride or pedal at a time.

CHAPTER 3

TOP TOURIST ATTRACTIONS IN REGENSBURG

Oh, the charming city of Regensburg, a treasure mine of history, culture, and architectural delights just waiting to be discovered.

As someone who has explored its historic streets and gazed at its beautiful landmarks, let me to be your guide to the top tourist attractions that distinguish Regensburg from other destinations.

Regensburg Cathedral (Dom. St. Peter)

Standing tall and strong against the Bavarian skyline, Regensburg Cathedral, also known as Dom St. Peter, exemplifies the city's rich religious legacy and architectural brilliance. As I entered this beautiful Gothic masterpiece, I was astonished by the grandeur of its interior, which was embellished with complex sculptures, spectacular stained glass windows, and awe-inspiring vaulted ceilings.

Don't miss the opportunity to climb the 105-meter-high south tower for panoramic views of the city and surrounding countryside - a really memorable experience that provides insight into Regensburg's history and present.

Old Stone Bridge (Steinerne Brücke)

The Old Stone Bridge, also known as Steinerne Brücke, crosses the peaceful waters of the Danube River and is a timeless reminder of Regensburg's medieval legacy. This ancient bridge, built in the 12th century, is one of Germany's oldest and has long served as an essential link between the city's two banks.

As I wandered across its ancient cobblestones, I couldn't help but image the innumerable tourists, traders, and pilgrims who had passed through this renowned landmark throughout the centuries. Pause midway to take in the amazing views of the river below, with the city skyline towering majestically on each side - a setting straight out of a medieval painting.

Thurn Und Taxis Palace

Prepare to be taken back in time as you enter the magnificent halls of the Thurn und Taxis Palace, a magnificent Baroque masterpiece located in Regensburg's center. Once the ancestral seat of the strong Thurn und Taxis noble family, this opulent mansion provides an intriguing peek into the lives of Bavaria's elite.

The Thurn und Taxis Palace oozes elegance and grandeur in every detail, from its magnificent ballrooms and finely painted bedrooms to its extensive gardens and picturesque courtyards. Take a guided tour to learn about the palace's rich history and the famous people who have walked its hallowed corridors.

Walhalla Memorial

Perched high above a hill overlooking the Danube River, the Walhalla Memorial is a magnificent memorial to Germany's great thinkers and cultural icons. This neoclassical monument, modeled after Athens' Parthenon, has busts and sculptures of approximately 130 prominent personalities from German history, including scientists, artists, philosophers, and statesmen.

As I went through the Walhalla's marble hallways, I was impressed by the atmosphere of awe and adoration. From Johann Wolfgang von Goethe to Albert Einstein, each bust serves as a reminder of the enormous contributions these individuals made to Germany's cultural and intellectual tapestry.

Saint Emmeram's Abbey (Schloss Thurn Und Taxis)

St. Emmeram's Abbey, commonly known as Schloss Thurn und Taxis, is a hidden treasure of Regensburg's architectural environment. Originally constructed as a monastery in the eighth century, the Thurn und Taxis family converted this huge complex into a beautiful palace, where they still live today.

As I wandered around the abbey's beautiful chapels, stately halls, and manicured gardens, I couldn't help but be struck by the medieval sanctuary's pure beauty and tranquillity. Don't miss out on a guided tour to learn about the abbey's rich history and the famous visitors who have passed through its halls throughout the years.

Historical Wurstkuchl

No trip to Regensburg is complete without enjoying the city's culinary pleasures, and the Historical Wurstkuchl is a must-see for foodies and history buffs both. Founded in 1135, this beautiful riverbank tavern claims to be the world's oldest sausage kitchen, having served classic Bavarian sausages and substantial food to hungry tourists for almost 800 years.

As I devoured my sizzling bratwurst and crunchy

sauerkraut overlooking the Danube, I couldn't help but feel a connection to the numerous tourists and residents who had dined in this ancient place before me. With its rustic beauty and delectable cuisine, the Historical Wurstkuchl is a real culinary institution that captures the spirit of Regensburg's rich culinary history.

Altes Rathaus (The Old Town Hall)

Nestled in the heart of Regensburg's picturesque Old Town, the Altes Rathaus, or Old Town Hall, is a stunning specimen of Gothic architecture that has endured the test of time. This ancient monument, with its unique exterior covered with bright paintings and artistic carvings, is both a visual feast for the eyes and a witness to the city's medieval magnificence.

Explore the Altes Rathaus's beautiful corridors, luxurious rooms, and finely decorated council chambers to learn about its rich past. Climb the tower for stunning views of the city below, with the Regensburg Cathedral's spires rising majestically in the distance.

Danube River Cruises

For an amazing experience, take a leisurely boat down the

Danube River and see Regensburg's stunning elegance from a different angle. Whether you choose a guided sightseeing tour or a romantic sunset cruise, a boat ride on the Danube provides exceptional views of the city's ancient cityscape, verdant riverbanks, and stunning bridges.

As I glided down the Danube's soothing currents, I couldn't help but feel a sense of calm wash over me, engulfing me in the timeless beauty of this historic waterway. From the landmark Old Stone Bridge to the serene riverside gardens, each curve along the river provided a fresh view of Regensburg's lovely surroundings.

Regensburg Museum Of History

The Regensburg Museum of History brings centuries of history and culture to life via immersive exhibitions and interactive displays.

This extensive museum, which includes ancient antiquities and archeological riches as well as medieval texts and Renaissance artworks, takes visitors on a fascinating tour through the city's history.

As I went around the museum's hallways, I was enthralled by the stories of Regensburg's great characters and significant historical events, from the Roman era to the present.

Don't miss the opportunity to examine the museum's enormous collection of antiquities, which includes rare coins, complex fabrics, and precious antiques that provide an insight into the life of previous generations.

Document Neupfarrplatz (Dokumentationszentrum Reichsparteitagsgelände)

Learn about one of the worst episodes in German history at the Document Neupfarrplatz, a moving monument and teaching center devoted to Nazi victims.

This mournful memorial, built on the site of a former synagogue destroyed during Kristallnacht, serves as a reminder of the crimes done against the Jewish people and other oppressed groups during the Holocaust.

As I strolled through the museum's eerie displays and mournful memorials, I was extremely inspired by the survival and perseverance tales of individuals who faced unfathomable suffering and persecution.

The Document Neupfarrplatz, with its stunning multimedia exhibits and eyewitness narratives, pays attention to the human cost of bigotry and prejudice, encouraging visitors to reflect on historical lessons and strive for a more equitable and compassionate society.

To summarize, Regensburg's best tourist sites provide a riveting combination of history, culture, and natural beauty that will delight tourists of all ages.

Each site, from the stately Regensburg Cathedral to the old Wurstkuchl Tavern, has its own narrative to tell and invites investigation and discovery.

So pack your luggage, ready to be inspired, and set off on an incredible adventure through Regensburg's historic streets.

CHAPTER 4

EXPLORING REGENSBURG'S OLD TOWN

Welcome to Regensburg's picturesque Old Town, where cobblestone alleys, medieval buildings, and vibrant market squares bring history to life. Allow me, as someone who has spent countless hours roaming these historical streets, to be your guide to Regensburg's historic core and its captivating attractions.

Wander around the medieval streets.

Step back in time as you explore through Regensburg's labyrinthine alleyways, where every corner has a story to tell. Lose yourself in the maze of small passageways dotted with centuries-old buildings, each with its own wounds and echoes from generations before.

As I walked around the cobblestone streets, I couldn't help but be amazed by the architectural marvels that surrounded me, from the high spires of the Regensburg Cathedral to the tiny half-timbered dwellings that appeared to lean perilously against one other. With each stride, I was transported to a bygone period, where knights patrolled the streets and merchants bartered over exotic products from other regions.

Discovering Hidden Gems

One of the most enjoyable aspects of touring Regensburg's Old Town is discovering hidden jewels - tucked-away courtyards, private gardens, and small squares that provide insight into the city's secret past and lively culture.

Take the opportunity to venture off the beaten road and uncover the gems that lie just beyond the tourist track.

During my excursions, I discovered hidden courtyards embellished with bright paintings, serene gardens blooming with fragrant blossoms, and secret tunnels leading to isolated squares where residents congregated to share stories and laughs.

Each discovery seemed like a tiny win, an opportunity to peel back the layers of history and reveal the mysteries of Regensburg's illustrious past.

Shopping In Old Town Markets

No trip to Regensburg's Old Town is complete without visiting its busy markets, where the sights, sounds, and scents of Bavaria come to life in a tornado of activity and excitement.

From traditional farmers' markets to artisanal craft fairs, there's something for everyone among the busy throng and vibrant stalls.

As I walked through the market squares, I couldn't help but be lured in by the brilliant colors and seductive fragrances that filled the air - the perfume of freshly baked bread, the sight of beautiful flowers in bloom, and the sound of merchants advertising their products in joyful Bavarian dialect.

Regensburg's markets, which range from handcrafted crafts and artisanal cheeses to locally produced fruit and specialty meats, are a feast for the senses as well as an opportunity to learn about the city's rich culinary history.

Trying Local Cuisine

After a day of touring Regensburg's Old Town, there's no

better way to relax than to sample the city's delectable food at one of its many lovely pubs, cafés, or beer gardens.

From hearty Bavarian classics to inventive culinary innovations, there's something for every taste and choice.

As the sun began to drop and the streets filled with the warm warmth of dusk, I was lured to a charming bar nestled away on a peaceful side street.

I relished typical Bavarian meals like crispy pig knuckle, creamy potato dumplings, and pungent sauerkraut, washed down with a delightful pint of locally produced beer.

Regensburg's culinary delights extend far beyond its hearty pub fare, with fine dining restaurants providing inventive gourmet cuisine and attractive cafés selling delectable pastries and fragrant coffees.

Don't pass up the opportunity to try local delicacies such as Regensburger Wurstsalat (sausage salad), Himmel und Erde (potatoes with apples and black pudding), or the city's famed Lebkuchen (gingerbread), which make excellent keepsakes to take home and enjoy long after your vacation is over.

Finally, touring Regensburg's Old Town is a journey of discovery and joy, with fresh adventures around every turn. Whether you're walking its ancient alleyways, discovering hidden jewels, shopping in its lively markets, or enjoying its delectable food, Regensburg's Old Town is a sensory feast and an opportunity to immerse yourself in the rich tapestry of Bavarian culture and history.

So tie up your walking shoes, ready to be delighted, and set off on an exciting adventure around Regensburg's old core.

CHAPTER 5

OUTDOOR ACTIVITIES IN AND AROUND REGENSBURG

The vast outdoors combines the beauty of nature with the excitement of adventure.

Regensburg and its surrounds provide several possibilities to immerse yourself in the stunning scenery and exciting activities that have made Bavaria such a popular destination for outdoor enthusiasts like myself.

Join me as we explore some of the greatest outdoor adventures Regensburg has to offer.

Hiking In The Bavarian Forest

Lace up your hiking boots and explore the untouched wildness of the Bavarian Forest, where ancient woods, flowing rivers, and craggy mountain peaks await.

This huge national park, located just a short drive from Regensburg, has a variety of hiking paths ideal for all ability levels, from leisurely strolls through calm forests to strenuous ascents to panoramic overlooks.

As I went along woodland pathways blanketed with pine needles and drenched with sunshine, I had a deep feeling of peacefulness and connectedness to the natural world.

With each step, I discovered hidden treasures: gurgling brooks alive with life, moss-covered boulders that seemed to speak ancient secrets, and towering trees that stretched silently to the skies.

For those looking for an adrenaline rush, the Bavarian Forest also offers mountain biking, rock climbing, and even animal watching.

Keep a watch out for elusive animals such as red deer, wild boar, and European lynx, who make this unspoiled environment home.

Cycling Along The Danube

For a more relaxing outdoor activity, jump on a bicycle and discover the staggering magnificence of the Danube River Cycle Path, one of Europe's most popular long-distance cycling routes.

This legendary track, which stretches over 600 kilometres from Germany's Black Forest to the Hungarian border, runs past gorgeous villages, rolling vineyards, and ancient cities, providing riders with an up-close view of the Danube's majesty.

As I traveled along the riverbank route, I was captivated by the ever-changing panoramas that unfurled before me, which ranged from verdant river valleys and sun-drenched meadows to breathtaking cliffs and historic castles perched high above the water.

The Danube Cycle Path, which includes authorized rest spots and attractive riverbank cafes, provides cyclists of all ages and abilities with the ideal balance of excitement and pleasure.

Danube River Activities (Canoeing, Kayaking, etc.)

The Danube River invites water enthusiasts looking for an adrenaline rush, with sports ranging from kayaking and canoeing to stand-up paddleboarding and white-water rafting. With its calm currents and picturesque surrounds, the Danube is the ideal playground for outdoor enthusiasts eager to test their talents and soak up the sun.

As I paddled over the beautiful waters of the Danube on a kayak, I felt a rush of pleasure and freedom that can only be experienced in the wild beauty of nature. With each paddle stroke, I discovered secret coves, jagged rapids, and serene backwaters, immersing myself in the river's timeless flow and the symphony of noises that surrounded me.

For those looking for a more relaxed experience, try taking a guided boat trip or sunset cruise along the Danube, where you can relax and enjoy the landscape while learning about the river's rich history and ecological significance from expert local guides.

Parks And Gardens In Regensburg

Back in the city, Regensburg has several green areas and urban oases where you may rest, unwind, and reconnect with nature among the rush and bustle of daily life. From lush parks and picturesque gardens to calm riverfront promenades, there are plenty of ways to escape the urban jungle and enjoy the great outdoors right in the middle of the city.

One of my preferred places for relaxation is Stadtamhof Park, a gorgeous green oasis on the Danube River's banks. Amidst fragrant flower beds and towering trees, you may take a leisurely stroll, have a picnic with friends, or simply sit back and soak in the tranquil environment while watching boats float past on the beautiful waters below.

For a more immersive botanical experience, visit the University of Regensburg's Botanical Garden, which has a vast array of plant species from all over the world. From exotic orchids and tropical palms to local wildflowers and medicinal plants, this calm sanctuary provides a sensory feast as well as an opportunity to escape the strains of daily life.

Finally, the outdoor activities in and around Regensburg provide several chances for adventure, discovery, and relaxation in the stunning landscapes of Bavaria. Whether you're hiking in the Bavarian Forest, riding along the Danube, canoeing along the river, or simply enjoying the city's natural areas, there's something for everyone in this outdoor paradise. So pack your luggage, embrace your adventurous spirit, and set off on a memorable excursion across Regensburg's natural beauties and environs.

CHAPTER 6

CULTURAL EXPERIENCES IN REGENSBURG

Oh, certainly, culture is the throbbing heart of each city, where history, art, and tradition combine to create a tapestry of beauty and significance.

Cultural opportunities abound in Regensburg, a city steeped in centuries of legacy and innovation, allowing visitors to immerse themselves in the city's rich creative and intellectual landscape.

Join me as we explore some of Regensburg's most memorable cultural experiences.

Attend A Classical Concert

Step inside Regensburg's ancient venues to experience the beauty of a classical performance, where soaring melodies and timeless masterpieces combine to create a symphony of music and emotion. Whether you're a seasoned fan or a newbie to classical music, attending a performance in Regensburg is an unforgettable experience.

As I took my place in the exquisite confines of the Thurn und Taxis Palace or the towering Regensburg Cathedral, I felt a rush of anticipation and excitement, knowing that I was about to see something very spectacular. From passionate symphonies and emotional sonatas to fascinating chamber music performances, each event was a sensory feast that allowed me to immerse myself in the music's amazing beauty.

Don't miss out on attending one of the city's renowned music festivals, such as the Regensburg Early Music Days or the Regensburg Jazz Weekend, when world-class performers from all over the world come together to celebrate the universal language of music and display their skills to enthusiastic audiences.

Visit Local Art Galleries And Museums

Regensburg has a rich cultural legacy that is represented in its various art galleries and museums, each of which offers a unique perspective on the city's past, present, and future. From ancient relics and medieval masterpieces to modern works by local artists, visitors of all ages and interests will find something to inspire and amuse.

As I went around the hallways of the Kunstforum Ostdeutsche Galerie or the Historisches Museum, I was enthralled by the vast assortment of artworks and objects on show, each expressing a narrative and encouraging interpretation. The treasures, which included bright paintings and sculptures as well as complex tapestries and ornamental arts, provided an intriguing glimpse into Regensburg's cultural and creative scene.

Be sure to visit the Stadtamhof town, which has a thriving arts scene with galleries, studios, and workshops showing the work of local artists and craftspeople. From traditional Bavarian crafts like pottery and woodworking to modern installations and avant-garde shows, the Stadtamhof community provides a diverse tapestry of artistic expression that will make an indelible impression.

Festival And Event Calendar

No visit to Regensburg is complete without experiencing its exciting festivals and events, which bring the city to life with music, dancing, and celebration all year. Regensburg has a variety of events for guests of all ages, including traditional folk festivals, medieval markets, modern art exhibits, and gourmet fairs.

The Regensburg Dult, a biennial folk festival held in the spring and fall, is a cultural landmark that draws tourists from near and far due to its vibrant atmosphere and festive attractions. From thrilling amusement rides and carnival games to traditional Bavarian music and hearty culinary delights, the Dult provides a taste of genuine Bavarian hospitality as well as an opportunity to experience the city's lively cultural traditions firsthand.

During the summer, don't miss the Regensburg Bürgerfest, a three-day street event that transforms the city's historic core into a hive of activity and excitement. From open-air concerts and theatrical performances to street food sellers and artisan stalls, the Bürgerfest has something for everyone, as well as an opportunity to celebrate Regensburg's cultural identity via the spirit of community and togetherness.

In conclusion, Regensburg's cultural experiences provide a rich tapestry of art, music, and culture that will fascinate and inspire tourists from near and far. Whether you're attending a classical symphony, touring local art galleries and museums, or celebrating at one of the city's bustling festivals, there are plenty of ways to immerse yourself in the cultural legacy of this charming Bavarian city. So pack your bags, ready to be amazed, and join us for an exciting adventure around Regensburg's cultural riches.

CHAPTER 7

DAY TRIPS FROM REGENSBURG

Oh, the joys of discovery! While Regensburg is a treasure mine of history and culture, there are several joys waiting to be discovered just outside its walls.

Join me as we go on a series of spectacular day adventures from Regensburg, each with its own distinct mix of adventure, beauty, and thrill.

Weltenburg Abbey And Danube Gorge

Our first visit is the lovely Weltenburg Abbey, located on the banks of the Danube River in the middle of the spectacular Danube Gorge. As we take a leisurely boat trip down the river, we are treated to stunning vistas of towering cliffs, lush woods, and tumbling waterfalls that border its banks.

When we arrive to Weltenburg Abbey, we are met by its exquisite Baroque exterior, which is filled with elaborate statues and detailed murals that depict the tale of its rich history.

When we walk inside, we are taken to a world of peace and reverence as we explore the abbey's majestic halls, magnificent chapels, and quiet gardens.

No visit to Weltenburg Abbey is complete without trying the famed Weltenburger Klosterbier, produced by monks using ancient methods passed down through centuries. We lift our glasses in honor of the abbey's enduring tradition and enjoy the rich, nuanced tastes of this cherished Bavarian beverage.

Nuremberg

Next, we travel to Nuremberg, a historic city where medieval charm meets modern elegance in a compelling fusion of past and present. As we walk through the city's cobblestone streets and lively market squares, we are taken back in time to the days of knights, merchants, and artists.

Our first trip is the magnificent Nuremberg Castle, which sits high above a rocky hill overlooking the city. From its tall walls, we have panoramic views of the city below, with red-roofed homes and historic churches spanning as far as the eye can see.

Descending from the castle, we make our way to the busy Hauptmarkt, where the sights and sounds of the city come to life in a flurry of bustle and enthusiasm. Among the bright booths and aromatic food kiosks, we try traditional dishes such as Nuremberg bratwurst and gingerbread, experiencing the aromas of this dynamic culinary scene.

Before we go, we'll stop at the iconic Nuremberg Trials courthouse, where the world came together to seek justice after World War II. Standing in the shadow of this solemn memorial, we ponder on historical lessons and the everlasting power of hope, resilience, and healing.

Munich

Our next stop is the bustling city of Munich, where

Bavarian history meets international flare in a dynamic combination of culture and innovation.

As we walk through the city's busy streets and attractive squares, we are met with ancient landmarks, exquisite boulevards, and lush green parks that dot the urban environment.

Our first stop is the renowned Marienplatz, the pulsating heart of Munich's historic center, where we are greeted by the imposing Neues Rathaus and its famed Glockenspiel, which comes to life with colourful figures and bells every noon.

We walk from Marienplatz to the huge Englischer Garten, one of the world's largest urban parks, where inhabitants and visitors alike enjoy the sun, picnicking by the river, and wandering among lush vegetation and calm lakes.

No visit to Munich is complete without experiencing the city's world-renowned beer culture, so we head to a typical beer garden and raise our steins in a toast to friendship, camaraderie, and the simple joys of life.

Salzburg, Austria

Our final day excursion brings us across the border to the wonderful city of Salzburg, Austria, where Mozart's music fills the air and baroque architecture catches the eye.

As we walk through the city's ancient streets and attractive squares, we are taken back to the Habsburg Empire's golden period.

Our first trip is the majestic Hohensalzburg Fortress, which sits high above a rocky slope overlooking the city. The towering battlements provide stunning views of the Salzach River and the snow-capped peaks of the Austrian Alps in the distance.

Descending from the citadel, we make our way to the lovely Altstadt, or Old Town, where we are met with exquisite palaces, gorgeous churches, and secret courtyards nestled in small passageways. Among the timeless beauty of Salzburg's historic core, we immerse ourselves in the city's rich cultural legacy, from its famous musical past to its dynamic arts scene.

Before leaving, we stop to pay our respects to the birthplace of Wolfgang Amadeus Mozart, the city's most renowned son. Standing in amazement in front of the humble home where the musical genius was born, we are reminded of the timeless power of creativity, passion, and inspiration to transcend time and place.

Neuschwanstein Castle

Our final journey takes us to the fairy-tale realm of Neuschwanstein Castle, hidden among the breathtaking peaks of the Bavarian Alps. As we travel through the lovely countryside, we are treated to stunning vistas of rolling hills, lush meadows, and clear lakes that reach as far as the eye can see.

We arrive to Neuschwanstein and are met by its towering turrets, soaring spires, and majestic architecture, which inspired Walt Disney and countless others throughout the world.

Stepping inside, we are taken to a world of enchantment and wonder as we explore the castle's grand hallways, luxurious chambers, and beautiful gardens, each more breathtaking than the previous.

Neuschwanstein Castle is a real masterpiece of romantic architecture, with its panoramic views and secret corridors, as well as its quirky décor and ageless appeal.

In conclusion, day trips from Regensburg provide several possibilities to explore, learn, and be inspired by the beauty and diversity of Bavaria and beyond.

Whether you're discovering ancient monuments, immersing yourself in cultural activities, or gazing at natural beauties, each day trip offers amazing memories and an opportunity to go on an adventure and discovery.

So pack your luggage, ready to be amazed, and go on a wonderful tour through Regensburg's attractions and environs.

CHAPTER 8

WHAT TO DO IN REGENSBURG

Regensburg is a city brimming with history, culture, and lively energy, with every corner telling a tale and every alleyway calling for adventure.

Join me as we discover the many joys that lie in this lovely Bavarian jewel, including guided walking tours, traditional Bavarian festivals, beer gardens, and nightlife hotspots.

Join A Guided Walking Tour

With a guided walking tour, you can go back in time and discover the mysteries of Regensburg's historic streets, as educated local guides bring the city's history and tradition to life right in front of your eyes. Whether you're a history buff, an architecture enthusiast, or simply want to learn more about the city's unique cultural tapestry, there's a walking tour for everyone.

As I embarked on a guided walking tour of Regensburg's Old Town, I was captivated by the stories of monarchs and knights, merchants and monks that rang through its cobblestone alleys.

From the stately Regensburg Cathedral to the ancient Stone Bridge and the picturesque Stadtamhof neighborhood, each monument unveiled a new chapter in the city's storied history and provided an opportunity to go back in time to a bygone age of medieval beauty.

Don't miss out on a themed walking tour, such as the Regensburg Beer Tour or the Night Watchman Tour, where costumed guides will take you on a journey through the city's beer-soaked history or tell you stories about ghosts, ghouls, and otherworldly spirits that haunt its shadowy alleyways.

Visit A Beer Garden

After a day of seeing Regensburg's ancient buildings, there's no better way to unwind than to soak up the sun and enjoy a delicious pint of beer at one of the city's famed beer gardens. Nestled within lush greenery and covered by thick chestnut trees, these outdoor oasis provide the ideal location for relaxation, socializing, and enjoying life's simple pleasures.

As I sat on a rustic wooden seat in the Thurn und Taxis Palace beer garden, I was struck by the convivial mood and the sight of both residents and visitors lifting their glasses in a toast to friendship, fraternity, and the delight of good company. With a nice, frothy beer in hand and laughing filling my ears, I felt a profound sense of satisfaction and belonging that can only be experienced in the warm embrace of a Bavarian beer garden.

Don't forget to try some classic Bavarian delicacies with your beer, such as pretzels, sausages, and substantial potato dumplings, which will excite your taste buds and leave you wanting more.

Attend A Traditional Bavarian Event

To experience real Bavarian culture and hospitality, visit one of the city's numerous traditional events and festivals, where music, dancing, and merriment reign supreme.

Regensburg has a variety of events for guests of all ages, from vibrant folk festivals and medieval markets to colorful parades and cultural celebrations.

The Regensburger Dult, a biennial folk festival held in the spring and fall, is a cultural landmark that draws tourists from all around with its bright atmosphere and joyful attractions. From thrilling amusement rides and carnival games to traditional Bavarian music and hearty culinary delights, the Dult provides a taste of genuine Bavarian hospitality as well as an opportunity to experience the city's lively cultural traditions personally.

During the summer, don't miss the Regensburger Bürgerfest, a three-day street event that transforms the city's historic core into a hive of activity and excitement. From open-air concerts and theatrical performances to street food sellers and artisan stalls, the Bürgerfest has something for everyone, as well as an opportunity to celebrate Regensburg's cultural identity via the spirit of community and togetherness.

Explore Regensburg's Nightlife

As the sun sets and the city comes alive with dazzling lights and throbbing energy, it's time to experience Regensburg's dynamic nightlife scene, which includes pubs, clubs, and live music venues that offer adventure and excitement.

Whether you choose a classy cocktail bar, a vibrant beer hall, or a noisy nightclub, there is a location to fit your taste and preferences.

As I wandered around Regensburg's lively Altstadt surroundings, I was spoilt for choice with its several taverns and pubs, each with its own distinct ambiance and assortment of beverages.

From quiet pubs selling traditional Bavarian beers to trendy cocktail bars creating inventive concoctions, the options and opportunities were infinite.

Don't miss out on seeing a live music performance at one of the city's many venues, where local and international musicians delight audiences with their unique sounds and contagious enthusiasm. From jazz and blues to rock and techno music, there is something for everyone's musical style and preference.

Finally, Regensburg has a diverse range of activities and experiences to suit every interest and inclination, from guided walking tours and beer garden excursions to traditional Bavarian festivities and boisterous nights out on the town.

So pack your bags, prepare to be amazed, and set off on an extraordinary tour through Regensburg's cultural pleasures, where each moment promises adventure, discovery, and the thrill of new experiences.

CHAPTER 9

WHAT NOT TO DO IN REGENSBURG

Welcome to Regensburg, a wonderful city. As someone who has walked these historic streets and witnessed the city's great hospitality directly, please allow me to provide some helpful advise on what not to do during your stay.

While Regensburg is a site of beauty, culture, and magic, it's also vital to be aware of local customs, rules, and safety measures to guarantee a pleasant and respectful visit to this Bavarian treasure.

Disrespect Local Customs And Traditions

First and foremost, you must respect the local community's customs and traditions throughout your stay in Regensburg. Regensburg, a city with a rich cultural legacy and a strong feeling of Bavarian identity, values particular traditions, including culinary practices, religious festivals, and folkloric events.

When entering stores, restaurants, or other facilities, be sure to greet individuals with a cheerful "Guten Tag" or "Servus". This little act of courtesy goes a long way toward demonstrating respect for the local culture and building relationships with the individuals you meet along the journey.

Similarly, while dining out or attending social functions, keep local etiquette in mind. For example, it is considered disrespectful to begin eating or drinking before everyone at the table has been served, so wait until everyone is seated and ready before digging into your meal.

Another cultural custom to be aware of is the practice of "quiet Sundays" in Germany, during which many stores and companies are closed and loud sounds or disruptions are typically discouraged. While Sundays are a great day to visit Regensburg's parks, museums, and historic monuments, it's crucial to keep noise levels down and respect the tranquil mood.

Ignore Public Transportation Rules

When it comes to traveling around Regensburg, the city's excellent public transit system provides a quick and environmentally responsible method to visit its numerous attractions and sites. There are several transportation alternatives available to meet the requirements and tastes of every tourist, including buses, trams, ferries, and bicycle rentals.
However, in order to have a safe and comfortable ride, you must first become acquainted with the norms and regulations of the public transportation system. To avoid fines or penalties, buy a ticket before boarding any kind of public transportation and verify it using the devices available.

Similarly, be aware of designated seating locations for elderly or disabled people, and be willing to surrender your seat to those in need. It's also crucial to keep noise to a minimal and avoid eating or drinking on buses and trams out of consideration for other passengers.

Litter Or Damage Historic Sites

Regensburg, a city with a rich history spanning over a thousand years, is home to a plethora of historic sites and landmarks that tell the narrative of its glorious past. From medieval churches and old barriers to scenic squares and quaint lanes, every aspect of the city is rich in history and legacy.

When visiting these historical places, it is critical to treat them with the care and respect they deserve. Avoid littering or leaving behind any rubbish, and avoid touching or harming any artifacts or buildings, no matter how appealing they may seem for a photo opportunity.

Similarly, be aware of any signs or barriers denoting restricted or off-limits portions of historical places. These places are frequently vulnerable or under repair, and breaking the regulations can result in irreversible harm to these valuable cultural artifacts.

Overlook Safety Precautions

Last but not least, make safety a priority throughout your stay in Regensburg. While the city is usually regarded as secure for tourists, it is always advisable to take common-sense precautions to safeguard yourself and your valuables.

For example, remain aware of your surroundings and keep a check on your belongings, particularly in popular tourist locations or on public transit. While visiting the city, consider wearing a money belt or carrying a secret bag to safeguard your passport, cash, and other critical papers.

Similarly, use caution when crossing busy streets or exploring new regions, and always obey traffic signals and pedestrian restrictions to avoid accidents or mishaps.

Finally, remain up to date on any local safety recommendations or emergency procedures, and don't be afraid to seek help from local authorities or tourist information centers if you have any difficulties or concerns during your visit.

To summarize, while Regensburg is a city of warmth, charm, and generosity, it's essential to be aware of local customs, norms, and safety measures to guarantee a pleasant and respectful voyage through this Bavarian jewel.

You'll have a memorable and enjoyable experience in Regensburg if you respect the city's traditions, follow public transportation rules, take care of historical sites, and prioritize safety at all times.

So, dear traveler, take these words of advice and set out on your tour through Regensburg's charming streets with confidence, kindness, and respect. Safe travels!

CHAPTER 10

ESSENTIAL TIPS FOR VISITORS

As you prepare to start on your adventure in the intriguing city of Regensburg, allow me to give some crucial suggestions to make your trip pleasant, fun, and memorable.

From learning basic German words to staying hydrated and sun-protected, these pointers will help you make the most of your time in this charming Bavarian jewel.

Learn Basic German Phrases

While many Regensburg residents understand English, learning a few basic German words will help you have a better travel experience and interact with the locals.

From greetings and pleasantries to asking for directions and buying meals, a few easy words may help you navigate the city confidently and comfortably.

For example, "Guten Tag" translates to "Good day" or "Hello," while "Bitte" means "Please" and "Danke" means "Thank you." Learning these fundamental greetings and expressions of thanks can help you respect the local culture and create connection with the people you meet on your travels.

Similarly, knowing how to ask for directions and order meals in German will allow you to easily traverse the city's busy streets and culinary pleasures.

Use sentences such as "Entschuldigung, wo ist...?" (Excuse me; where is...?) and "Ich hätte gerne..." (I would like...) to successfully explain your requirements and preferences while you explore Regensburg.

Respect Quiet Hours

In Germany, particularly in residential areas and communities, quiet hours are set aside during the day and night to keep noise levels to a minimum. These calm hours are normally between 1:00 and 3:00 p.m., then again from 10:00 p.m. to 6:00 a.m., however they may differ depending on the area.

Be aware of noise levels during these quiet hours to demonstrate respect for the local community and to create a calm atmosphere for both locals and fellow guests. Avoid playing loud music, exhibiting unruly behavior, or producing excessive noise, especially in shared accommodations such as hotels or vacation rentals.

Similarly, adhere to noise regulations in public spaces like parks, squares, and outdoor sitting areas, where both locals and tourists cherish calm pleasure. By reducing noise to a minimum during quiet hours, you may assist to maintain the city's calm and harmony while also fostering a strong connection with the local community.

Carry Cash For Smaller Purchase

While credit and debit cards are generally accepted in Regensburg, especially at bigger places such as hotels, restaurants, and stores, it is always a good idea to have some cash on hand for minor purchases and transactions.

Many smaller establishments, street sellers, and local markets may only take cash payments, so having some euros on hand might save you time and trouble when traveling.

Furthermore, certain companies may require a minimum purchase quantity for card transactions, so having cash on hand might save you from any difficulty or additional charges. To avoid loss or theft, withdraw cash from ATMs or banks before beginning your travels in Regensburg, and keep your money secure in a travel wallet or money belt.

Stay Hydrated And Sun Protected

Regensburg has a moderate climate, with pleasant summers and cold winters, making it an excellent choice for outdoor activities and tourism. However, it is critical to keep hydrated and sun-protected, especially during the summer months when temperatures can soar and the sun's rays are strong.

Bring a filled water bottle with you while you explore the city, and take frequent stops to hydrate and relax in shaded areas or air-conditioned buildings. To protect yourself from the sun's damaging UV rays, consider wearing lightweight, breathable clothes, a wide-brimmed hat, and sunglasses, as well as applying sunscreen with a high SPF rating to exposed skin.

Furthermore, be aware of the symptoms of heat exhaustion or dehydration, such as dizziness, lethargy, and increased thirst, and seek shade and cold temperatures if you begin to feel sick. Staying hydrated and sun-protected will allow you to enjoy Regensburg's attractions without succumbing to the heat or discomfort of the summer sun.

Finally, these vital Regensburg tourist advice will help you traverse the city with confidence, kindness, and respect, resulting in a smooth and delightful journey through this lovely Bavarian treasure. From learning basic German words to respecting quiet hours, bringing cash for modest purchases, and being hydrated and sun-protected, these pointers will help you make the most of your time in Regensburg and create amazing experiences that last a lifetime. So, dear tourist, hear these words of encouragement and set out on your tour through Regensburg's streets with confidence, curiosity, and an adventurous attitude. Safe travels!

CHAPTER 11

ITINERARIES FOR DIFFERENT KINDS OF TRAVELERS

Oh sure, dear visitor, whether you're looking for a weekend getaway, a cultural immersion, an outdoor adventure, a family-friendly excursion, or a low-budget trip, Regensburg has something for everyone.

Join me as I create custom itineraries for each type of visitor, ensuring that your stay in this charming Bavarian city is nothing short of wonderful.

Weekend Getaway

A weekend visit to Regensburg offers leisure, romance, and renewal among the city's historic charm and picturesque splendor. Here's a suggested itinerary to make the most of your brief but lovely trip:

Friday Evening:

Arrive in Regensburg and settle into your lovely lodging in the Old Town. Take a leisurely stroll along the Danube River's banks to view the sunset, which casts a golden light over the city's gorgeous cityscape.

Enjoy a romantic meal at one of Regensburg's lovely restaurants, where you may eat traditional Bavarian cuisine combined with good wine or beer.

After supper, go for a moonlit walk around the illuminated streets of the Old Town, taking up the atmosphere of this beautiful city beneath the stars.

Saturday:

Begin the day with a substantial Bavarian breakfast at a neighborhood café or bakery. Sample freshly made bread, pastries, and other wonderful goodies. Prepare for a day of discovery and adventure!

Take a guided walking tour of Regensburg's historic sites, which include the magnificent Regensburg Cathedral, the renowned Stone Bridge, and the attractive Stadtamhof surrounding area. Wandering around the city's cobblestone streets and secret passageways, you may learn about its rich history and traditions.

In the afternoon, spend time at one of Regensburg's numerous museums or art galleries, where you may learn about the city's cultural riches and masterpieces.

Alternatively, enjoy a picturesque boat tour along the Danube River and admire the breathtaking panoramic views of the city and its surrounds.

Sunday:

Indulge in a leisurely breakfast at a local café or bistro. Enjoy wonderful brunch dishes and specialty coffees while immersing yourself in Regensburg's laid-back café culture. Take your time relaxing and unwinding before saying goodbye to this wonderful city and returning home, refreshed and revitalized by your weekend trip.

Cultural Immersion

A cultural immersion experience in Regensburg provides a fascinating tour through the city's rich past and artistic legacy for those who are interested in history, art, or culture. Here's a recommended schedule to help you dive deeply into the cultural richness of this Bavarian gem:

Day 1:

Begin your cultural immersion by seeing Regensburg Cathedral, a Gothic masterpiece that represents the city's spiritual and cultural legacy. As you go through its sacred hallways and chapels, see its soaring spires, beautiful stained glass windows, and elaborate sculptures.

Next, walk through the streets of Old Town to see the city's many historic sites, such as the Old Stone Bridge, the Altes Rathaus (Old Town Hall), and the Historical Wurstkuchl, one of the world's oldest sausage cookers. Wander through Regensburg's convoluted lanes and lovely squares to experience the city's medieval charm.

In the afternoon, go to the Regensburg Museum of History or the Kunstforum Ostdeutsche Galerie, where you may see a broad collection of artworks and objects that highlight the city's cultural past and creative tradition. From ancient relics and medieval treasures to modern masterpieces, there is something for every art enthusiast to appreciate.

Day 2:

Enjoy Regensburg's lively cultural scene by attending a classical music or theatrical play at one of the city's historic venues. There are plenty of cultural opportunities to amuse and inspire, including rousing symphonies and opera performances, avant-garde theater, and modern dance.

Don't pass up the opportunity to attend one of Regensburg's numerous traditional festivals and events, where you may immerse yourself in the city's folkloric traditions and cultural festivities. Whether it's the Regensburger Dult, the Bürgerfest, or the Christmas market, these colorful gatherings allow you to feel the genuine essence of Regensburg and its residents.

Outdoor Adventure

Regensburg provides several chances for outdoor enthusiasts and nature lovers to discover the area's spectacular natural landscapes and visual splendor. Here's a proposed schedule to get you started on an outdoor trip in and around the city:

Day 1:

Begin your outdoor experience with a stroll in the Bavarian Forest, where you may discover lush woods, beautiful lakes, and craggy mountain summits. Choose from a selection of hiking paths, ranging from short walks to strenuous excursions, and immerse yourself in nature's peace and beauty.

In the afternoon, set off on a cycling tour along the Danube River, where you may ride along gorgeous bike trails while admiring the stunning views of the river valley and surrounding countryside. Stop along the route to see picturesque villages, visit historic landmarks, and have a picnic lunch in the heart of the Bavarian countryside.

Day 2:

Enjoy a kayaking or canoeing adventure on the Danube River. Explore magnificent gorges, placid waters, and lush riverbanks. Whether you're a novice or an expert paddler, there are several opportunities to appreciate the natural beauty of the river and its environs.

After your water experience, visit one of Regensburg's numerous parks and gardens to rest and unwind amidst lush greenery, vibrant flowers, and quiet ponds. Take a leisurely stroll, have a picnic lunch, or simply appreciate the beauty of nature while soaking up the sun and fresh air.

Family-Friendly Trip

Regensburg has a variety of family-friendly activities and attractions to keep everyone interested and involved. Here's a sample itinerary to help you arrange a memorable and fun trip with your loved ones.

Day 1:

Begin your family-friendly excursion with a visit to the Walhalla Memorial, which has spectacular architecture, expansive views, and busts of prominent characters from German history. Explore the neighboring gardens and have a picnic lunch in the beautiful Bavarian countryside.

In the afternoon, go on a Danube River tour to experience a lovely boat trip down the river while taking in panoramic views of Regensburg and the surrounding area. Choose from a range of cruise activities, such as sightseeing tours, sunset cruises, and family-friendly themed excursions.

Day 2:

Visit the Regensburg Museum of Natural History to learn about science and technology via interactive exhibitions, hands-on activities, and live demonstrations suitable for all ages. Everyone can enjoy everything from dinosaur fossils and meteorites to interactive astronomy and environmental displays.

After your museum tour, spend the afternoon visiting the Stadtamhof surrounding area, where you can stroll through picturesque streets, explore local stores, and have ice cream or gelato at one of the numerous adorable cafés and dessert shops. Don't pass up the opportunity to visit the Stadtamhof Playground, where kids may burn off energy and meet new friends while parents rest and unwind.

Budget Travel

Regensburg has plenty of reasonable and fun adventures that won't break the wallet. Here's a recommended schedule to help you get the most of your vacation while staying within your budget:

Day 1:

Begin your budget-friendly vacation with a self-guided walking tour of Regensburg's Old Town. Explore historic sites, quaint lanes, and gorgeous squares at your own leisure for free. Don't forget to download a free audio guide or grab a map from the tourist information center to assist you navigate the city's streets and sights.

In the afternoon, take a picnic lunch and travel to one of Regensburg's attractive parks or green spaces, such as the Stadtpark or Donaupark, to enjoy a leisurely meal surrounded by thick foliage and lovely landscape. Take advantage of free outdoor activities such as walking, running, or simply resting in nature while admiring the beauty of Regensburg's outdoor areas.

Day 2:

Explore Regensburg's free museums and cultural

attractions, including the Historisches Museum and the Kunstforum Ostdeutsche Galerie. These exhibits offer a diverse collection of artworks and artifacts without cost. Many museums provide free entry on specific days or give special rates to students, seniors, and other groups, so check their websites or ask at the ticket counter for additional information.

After your museum visit, take a self-guided walking tour through Regensburg's rich street art culture, which includes vivid murals and graffiti artworks. As you walk around the city's urban landscape, you'll see and discover everything from playful street art works to thought-provoking political messages.

Finally, whether you're looking for a weekend break, a cultural immersion experience, an outdoor adventure, a family-friendly trip, or a low-cost visit, Regensburg has something for everyone. By following these bespoke itineraries and taking advantage of the unique experiences that await you in this lovely Bavarian city, you'll make memories that last a lifetime and leave a piece of your heart in Regensburg. So pack your luggage, get ready to be amazed, and start on an incredible tour through the delights of this ancient and bustling city. Safe travels, dear traveler, and may your experiences in Regensburg be as enjoyable as they are different!

CHAPTER 12

ACCOMMODATION

The search for the ideal spot to lay one's weary head in the charming city of Regensburg! As someone who has strolled these ancient streets and taken sanctuary in its friendly lodgings, please allow me to guide you through the various alternatives accessible to guests looking for a place to call home during their stay.

From luxury resorts to low-cost hotels, boutique guesthouses, and one-of-a-kind stays, this Bavarian jewel has something for everyone's taste and budget.

Overview Of Accommodation Options

Regensburg has a broad range of hotel alternatives to meet the requirements and tastes of every tourist.

Whether you like luxurious luxury, warm comfort, or quirky charm, you'll discover a variety of options to fit your taste and budget.

Luxury Resorts

Regensburg's finest resorts and hotels provide exceptional service, rich facilities, and spectacular vistas for tourists seeking ultimate comfort, indulgence, and relaxation.

These upmarket establishments guarantee a wonderful stay, with magnificent accommodations and gourmet restaurants, as well as spa facilities and recreational activities.

Budget-Friendly Hotels

Regensburg offers inexpensive hotels and guesthouses that provide clean, pleasant rooms without breaking the bank. With a variety of alternatives to select from, such as chain hotels, family-run guesthouses, and low-cost hostels, you're sure to find a location that meets your requirements and budget.

Boutique Guesthouses:

Boutique guesthouses and bed-and-breakfasts provide a personalized and private experience, with charm, character, and genuine hospitality. Set in historic houses or beautiful neighborhoods, these one-of-a-kind hotels provide warm lodgings, handmade meals, and personalized care to make you feel right at home.

Unique Stays:

Regensburg provides a range of interesting housing alternatives, including restored historic buildings, floating hotels, eco-friendly cottages, and treehouses. Whether you want a taste of history, a connection with nature, or a touch of whimsy, Regensburg has a one-of-a-kind experience for you.

Top Recommended Hotels And Resorts

As someone who has personally experienced Regensburg's warmth and generosity, please allow me to propose a few exceptional hotels and resorts that have received wonderful ratings from both visitors and locals:

Hotel Orphee: Located in the center of Regensburg's Old Town, Hotel Orphee provides magnificent accommodations, outstanding service, and a prominent position within walking distance of the city's main attractions.

ACHAT Plaza Herzog am Dom: This modern hotel has big rooms, good facilities, and breathtaking views of the medieval cathedral, making it a popular among tourists looking for comfort and convenience.

Hotel Goliath am Dom: With its attractive courtyard, pleasant rooms, and friendly staff, Hotel Goliath am Dom emanates warmth and welcome, serving as a delightful home away from home in the center of the city.

Sorat Insel-Hotel Regensburg: Located on an island in the Danube River, this one-of-a-kind hotel provides serene settings, stunning views, and easy access to the city center, making it a great choice for tourists looking for peace and quiet.

Altstadthotel Arch: Housed in a historic structure from the 12th century, Altstadthotel Arch mixes old-world elegance with modern amenities, providing guests with a genuinely unique and unforgettable stay in Regensburg's Old Town.

Choosing The Right Accommodation For You

When it comes to finding the best place to stay in Regensburg, you need consider numerous variables such as location, budget, facilities, and personal preferences. Here are some pointers to help you select the best option for your needs:

Consider the Location: Consider your accommodation's location and closeness to the city's major attractions, restaurants, and transit choices when deciding whether you want to be in the middle of the action or away from it all.

Set a Budget: Determine how much you are prepared to spend on accommodations and select a place that suits your budget while still providing the facilities and services you require.

Check Reviews: Before reserving your accommodation, check previous guests' reviews to get a feel of their experiences and satisfaction levels. Look for places that have received consistently favorable feedback and high ratings to ensure a comfortable visit.

Consider Amenities: Consider the facilities and services that are essential to you, such as free Wi-Fi, included breakfast, on-site parking, or a fitness facility, and select a property that provides the amenities you require for a comfortable and pleasurable stay.

Finally, follow your intuition and select a property that seems appropriate to you. Whether you like the charm of a boutique guesthouse, the elegance of a five-star resort, or the warmth of a low-cost hotel, trust your instincts and choose what feels right for you.

Bookkeeping Tips & Tricks

Once you've decided on the ideal hotel for your stay in Regensburg, here are a few pointers to assist you get the greatest value and a simple booking process:

Book in Advance: To ensure the greatest pricing and availability, book your accommodations well in advance, especially during peak travel seasons or for major events and festivals.

Look for Deals and Discounts: Hotels and booking websites may offer special deals, discounts, and promotions, such as early booking discounts, last-minute deals, or package offerings that include lodging and other facilities.

Consider Alternative Booking Platforms: In addition to typical booking services, try Airbnb, HomeAway, or Booking.com to uncover unusual lodgings and cheap rates that may not be accessible elsewhere.

Be Flexible With Your Dates: If feasible, change your trip dates to take advantage of reduced rates and more availability. Consider going during off-peak seasons or midweek to get the greatest rates on accommodations.

Contact The Hotel Directly: Contacting the hotel directly may result in lower rates or additional incentives, such as complimentary upgrades or late check-out. Do not hesitate to contact the hotel's bookings staff to learn about any special discounts or promotions that may be available.

To summarize, selecting the ideal hotel in Regensburg is a pleasant trip in itself, with a plethora of possibilities to suit every taste, budget, and preference.

Whether you're looking for luxury and pleasure, comfortable comfort, or a one-of-a-kind and unforgettable experience, this lovely Bavarian city will welcome you with open arms.

So pack your luggage, find your chosen hotel, and ready to go on a voyage of discovery and enjoyment through Regensburg's medieval streets. Dear traveler, safe travels, and may your stay be as lovely as the city itself!

Conclusion

As I say goodbye to the charming city of Regensburg, I can't help but dwell on the many gems I've discovered throughout my stay. Regensburg has left an unforgettable stamp on my heart, from the grandeur of its ancient structures to the beauty of its cobblestone streets, and I am grateful for the memories I have made here.

Recap Of Regensburg Highlights

Regensburg Cathedral, with its soaring spires and stunning architecture, represents the city's rich history and cultural legacy. Exploring its solemn corridors and chapels took me back in time, and I was astounded by the grandeur and craftsmanship of this Gothic masterpiece.

The Old Stone Bridge, which spans the Danube River, provided panoramic views of the city's skyline and served as a magnificent background for leisurely walks and romantic sunset walks. Crossing its ancient arches, I felt a kinship to the ancestors that came before me, their footsteps resonating through time.

Thurn und Taxis Palace, with its magnificent interiors and groomed grounds, offered an insight into the lives of Bavaria's upper class. Wandering around its beautiful halls and lush gardens, I was transported to a world of grandeur and excess, with every detail indicating riches and privilege.

St. Emmeram's Abbey, set in the rolling hills of the Bavarian countryside, conveyed a sense of calm and peace that spoke to my spirit. Exploring its tranquil cloisters and beautiful gardens, I found refuge in the beauty of nature and the stillness of thought.

Of course, no visit to Regensburg is complete without sampling the city's gastronomic pleasures. From hearty Bavarian meals to exquisite pastries and luscious sweets, the city's eateries and cafés were a sensory feast that left me wanting more.

Farewell And Happy Travels

As I prepare to continue my journey, I am reminded of Regensburg's beauty, history, and kindness, as well as the feeling that I have been touched by something genuinely wonderful. To everyone who explore its streets and marvel at its beauties, I bid you farewell and best wishes for safe travels on your own journeys.

May the spirit of Regensburg accompany you wherever you go, leading you down pathways of discovery and filling your heart with joy and amazement. Farewell, my friend, amidst the old spires and meandering alleyways of this Bavarian beauty, and may your travels be as lovely as the city itself.

Appendix: Useful Resources

Dear traveler, as you prepare to embark on your journey to the enchanting city of Regensburg, please allow me to provide you with a treasure trove of important information to enrich your vacation and ensure a seamless and unforgettable experience. From emergency contacts to navigational tools, supplemental reading, and handy local words, consider this your essential guide to explore Regensburg's marvels with comfort and confidence.

Emergency Contacts

In the unusual case of an emergency during your stay in Regensburg, you must have access to the necessary contacts for aid and support. Here are some important emergency numbers and contacts to have handy:

Emergency Services:

Police: 110

Fire Department: 112

Medical Emergency: 112

Embassies and Consulates:

United States Embassy in Berlin: +49 30 83050

United Kingdom Consulate in Munich: +49 89 211090

Australian Embassy in Berlin: +49 30 8800880

Canadian Embassy in Berlin: +49 30 203120

24-Hour Pharmacies:

Apotheke am Theater, Theatergasse 2: +49 941 52484

Apotheke im Donau Einkaufszentrum, Weichser Weg 5: +49 941 306262

Tourist Information Center

Regensburg Tourismus GmbH, Altes Rathaus, Rathausplatz 4: +49 941 5074410

Maps And Navigational Tools

Navigating Regensburg's meandering streets and ancient sites may be an adventure in and of itself, but don't worry, dear visitor, there are lots of maps and navigational aids to help you find your way about. Here are some crucial resources to help you in your explorations:

City Maps

Pick up a free city map at the tourist information center or your hotel to help you navigate Regensburg's streets and find significant attractions, restaurants, and monuments.

Mobile Applications:

Download navigation applications for your smartphone, like as Google Maps or Maps.me, to get real-time directions, offline maps, and places of interest as you explore Regensburg by foot or by public transportation.

Walking Tours:

Join a guided walking tour of Regensburg's Old Town to uncover hidden jewels and historic sites, as well as learn about the city's rich history and culture from expert local guides.

Additional Reading And References

There are several resources accessible for people interested in learning more about Regensburg's history, culture, and attractions. Here are some recommended books, websites, and articles to help you along your journey:

Books:

"Regensburg: A Detailed Architectural Guide" by Hubert F. Schmitt

"Regensburg: UNESCO World Heritage City" by Wolfgang Gleissner

"The History of Regensburg" by Karl Bauer

Websites:

Regensburg Tourism Official Website: www.regensburg.de/tourismus

UNESCO World Heritage Website: whc.unesco.org/en/list/1155

Articles:

"10 Must-See Attractions in Regensburg" by Travel + Leisure

"Exploring Regensburg: A Journey Through Time" by National Geographic

"The Culinary Delights of Regensburg" by Conde Nast Traveler

Useful Local Phrases

Finally, dear tourist, by learning a few key words in German, you may immerse yourself in the local culture and interact with the Regensburg people. While many locals understand English, making an attempt to converse in their original language is always welcomed and may improve your overall trip experience. Here are a few helpful sentences to get you started:

Greetings:

Hello: Hallo

Good morning: Guten Morgen

Good afternoon: Guten Tag

Good evening: Guten Abend

Goodbye: Auf Wiedersehen

Basic Phrases:

Yes: Ja

No: Nein

Please: Bitte

Thank you: Danke schön

You're welcome: Bitte schön

Directions:

Where is...?: Wo ist...?

Excuse me, can you help me?: Entschuldigung, können Sie mir helfen?

I'm lost: Ich habe mich verirrt

Dining:

I would like...: Ich hätte gerne...

The bill, please: Die Rechnung, bitte

Cheers!: Prost!

With these essential resources at your fingertips, dear traveler, you are well-equipped to embark on a journey of discovery through the historic streets and scenic landscapes of Regensburg. May your adventures be filled with wonder, joy, and unforgettable experiences as you explore this Bavarian jewel and create memories to last a lifetime. Safe travels, dear friend, and may the spirit of Regensburg guide you on your path wherever it may lead.

Printed in Great Britain
by Amazon